BIG IDEA

FLIGHT

Les Asselstine

SERIES EDITORS

Jim Cummins • David Freeman • Yvonne Freeman
Les Asselstine • Catherine Little

PEARSON

Pearson Canada Inc.
26 Prince Andrew Place
Don Mills, ON M3C 2T8
Customer Service: 1-800-361-6128

Rubicon
www.rubiconpublishing.com

We acknowledge the financial support of the Government of Canada.

Canada

Associate Publisher: Cheryl Turner
Editor: Lauren Wing
Editorial Assistant: Vicky He
Creative Director: Jennifer Drew
Designers: Sherwin Flores, Robin Forsyth, Brandon Koepke

18 19 20 21 22 6 5 4 3 2

ISBN: 978-1-77058-736-6

Paper used in the production of this book is a natural, recyclable product made from wood grown in sustainable forests. The manufacturing process conforms to the environmental regulations of the country of origin.

Printed in China

BIG IDEA

CONTENTS

Exploring Flight

BIG IDEA Animals and machines use air to fly.

Think about things that fly. How are they the same? How are they different?

How can air be used to fly?

CHAPTER 1

AIR

Air is made of different gases. The gases are made of tiny parts. These tiny parts are called molecules.

Air close to Earth is thick. The gas molecules are close together. Humans can breathe this air. Many birds fly low in the thick air.

Air high above Earth is thin. The gas molecules are far apart. It is hard to breathe in thin air. Big airplanes can fly high in the thin air.

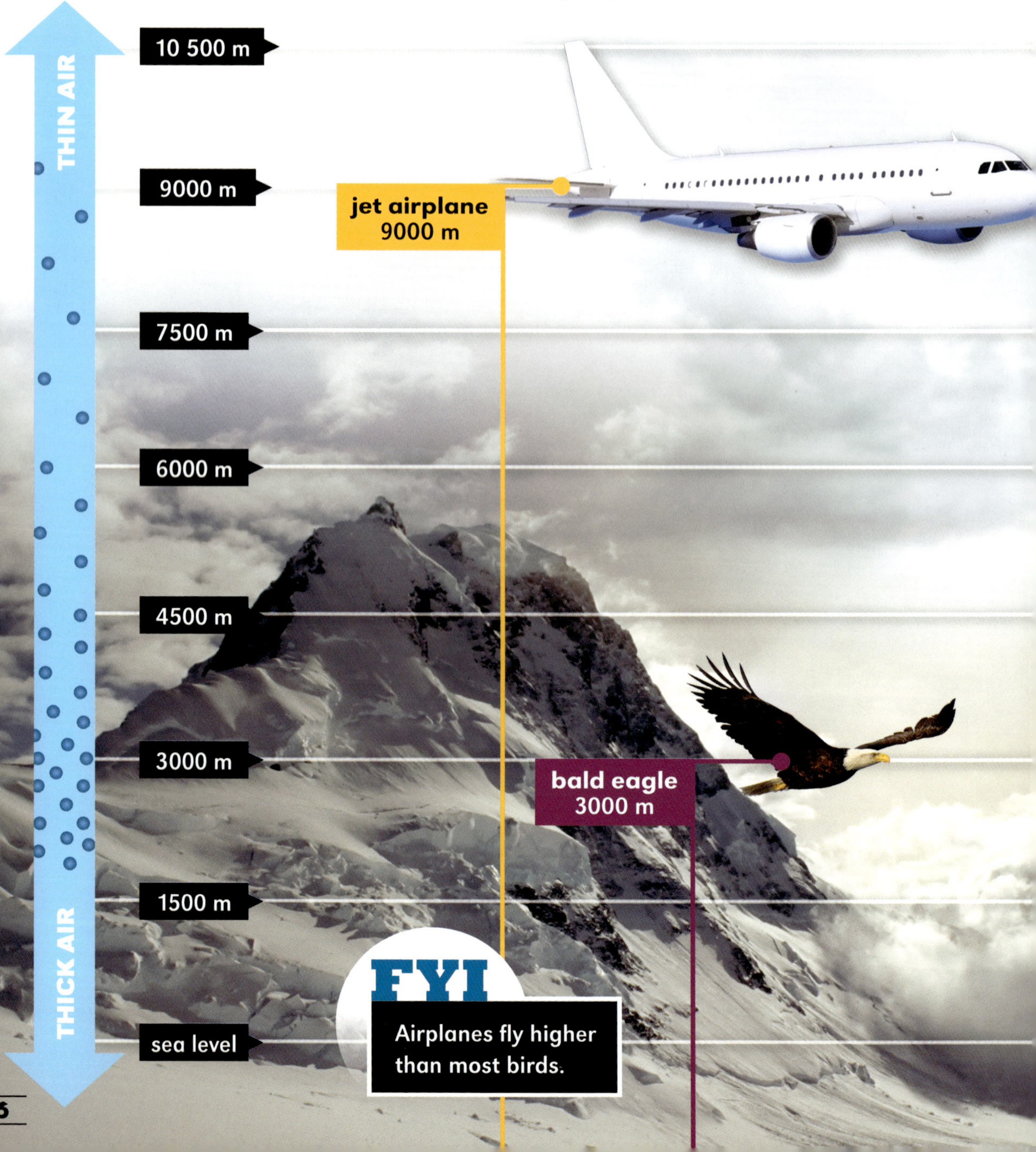

FYI

Airplanes fly higher than most birds.

BIG IDEA Air changes at different heights above Earth.

Air is made up mostly of nitrogen and oxygen.

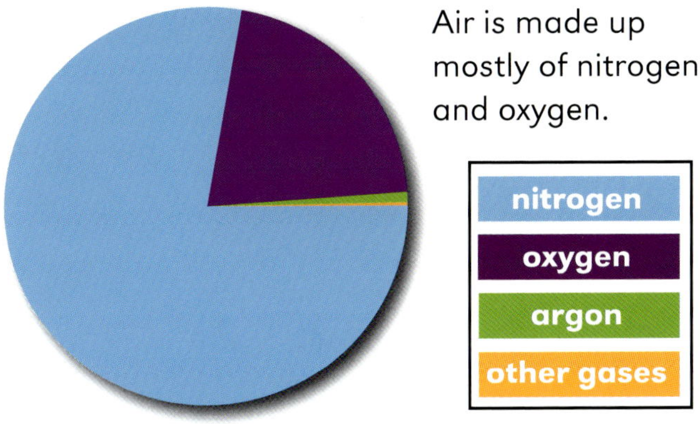

1. Why is air important?
2. How is air close to Earth different from air high above Earth?

Properties of Air

BIG IDEA Air has properties.

People can make flying machines if they know the properties of air. Properties are how something looks or acts. Here are four properties of air.

1. Air takes up space.
2. Air has mass.
3. Air spreads out when it is hot.
4. Air has pressure. This means it pushes against things, including you.

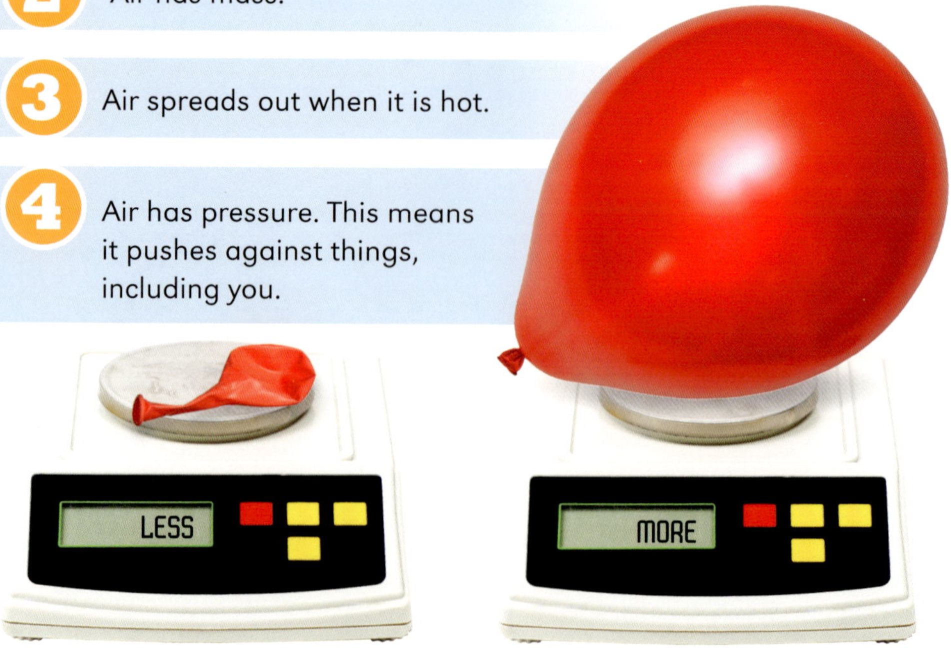

The balloon weighs more with air inside.
This is because air has mass. It also takes up space.

FYI

Some machines push air into a small space. The air molecules are pushed together. This is called air compression. Jet engines on airplanes compress air. When the compressed air is pushed out of the back of the engine, it makes the airplane go forward.

The molecules in hot air do not act the same as the molecules in cold air.

HOT AIR: Light

The molecules in hot air are far apart.

Molecules that are far apart make hot air less dense. This means fewer molecules fill the space.

Hot air is less dense than cold air. This makes hot air light.

Hot air moves up above cold air.

COLD AIR: Heavy

The molecules in cold air are close together.

Molecules that are close together make cold air dense. This means that more molecules fill the space.

Cold air is denser than hot air. This makes cold air heavy.

Cold air moves down below hot air.

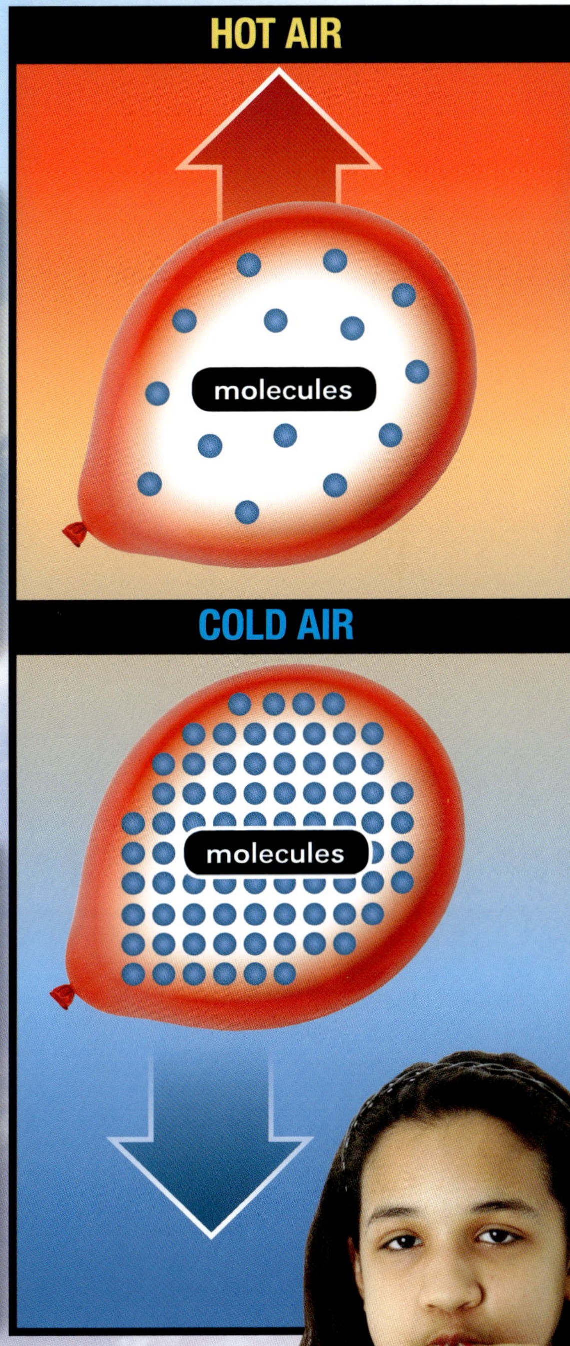

1. Why does a balloon weigh more with air in it?

2. Why does hot air rise above cold air?

Using Air to Fly

BIG IDEA People use the properties of air to fly machines.

People use the properties of air to fly a hot-air balloon. There is hot air inside the balloon. The hot air rises above the cold air in the sky. This makes the balloon fly.

1

The hot-air balloon is spread out on the ground.

2

Big fans fill the balloon with air.

3

The hot-air balloon has a burner.
The burner uses fuel to make the air hot.

4

The air inside the balloon gets hot. The hot air starts to rise. The hot air makes the balloon rise with it. The balloon moves with the wind.

5

The pilot opens a vent in the balloon. The vent lets out some of the hot air. The air inside the balloon cools down. The balloon goes down to the ground.

?

1. Why does the balloon rise?
2. What makes the balloon go back down?

ACTIVITY 1

SHOW HOW HOT AIR RISES

Work with a partner to show how hot air is lighter than cold air.

YOU WILL NEED

paper lunch bags

tape

string

lamp with light bulb

metre stick

1 Tie a piece of string to the metre stick at 50 cm.

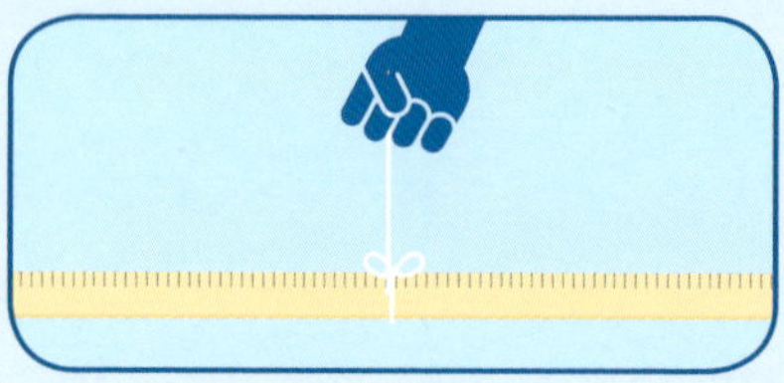

2 Tape another piece of string to the bottom of one lunch bag.

3 Tie the other end of the string on the bag to one end of the metre stick.

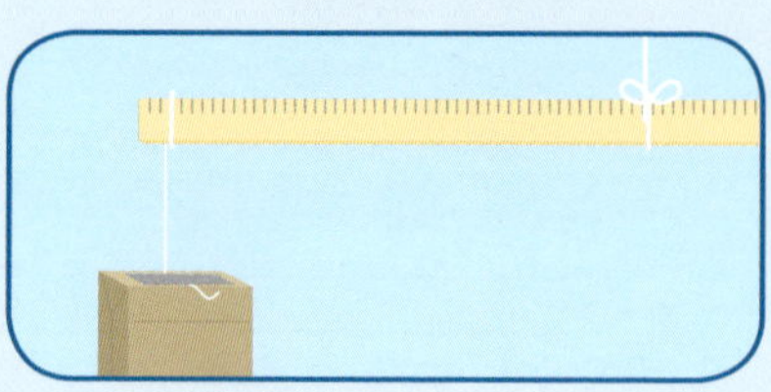

4 Repeat steps 2 and 3 using the other lunch bag.

BE SAFE

Do not hold the paper bag against the light bulb. It might burn.

5 Have one person hold the string attached at 50 cm on the metre stick. Make sure the metre stick is balanced.

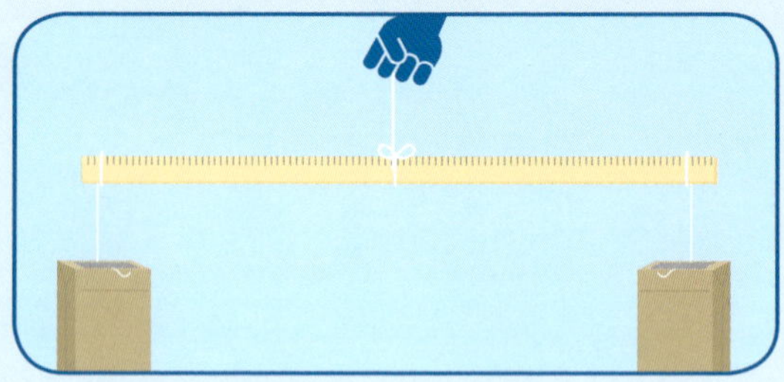

6 Predict what will happen when you put the light bulb under one bag. Record your prediction.

7 Turn on the light bulb. Put the light bulb under one bag. Do not touch the bag with the light bulb.

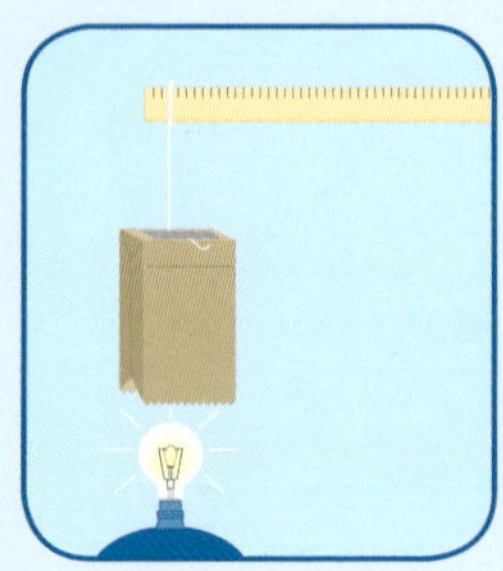

8 Record your observations.

ANALYZE & REFLECT

1. What have you learned that helped you to make your prediction?
2. What did the light bulb do to the air in the bag?

ACTIVITY 2

MEASURE AIR MASS

Use balance to show that air has mass.

YOU WILL NEED

chairs

tape pump string pin balloons

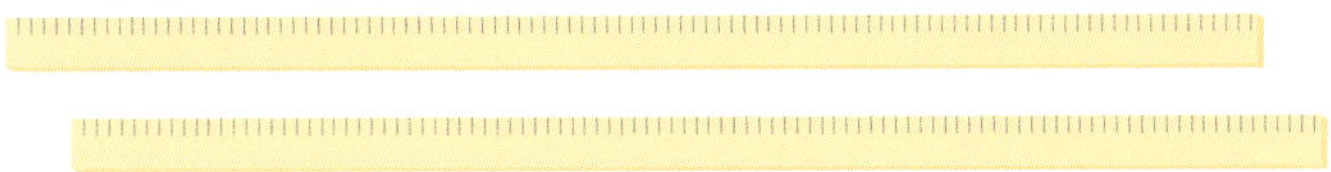

metre sticks

1 Put two chairs almost 1 m apart.

2 Put the first metre stick on top of the chairs. Tape the metre stick to the chairs.

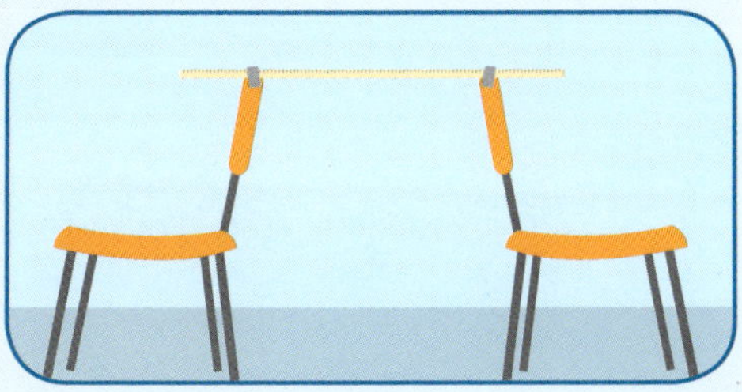

3 Tie the second metre stick to the first metre stick at 50 cm. Use a 20 cm piece of string.

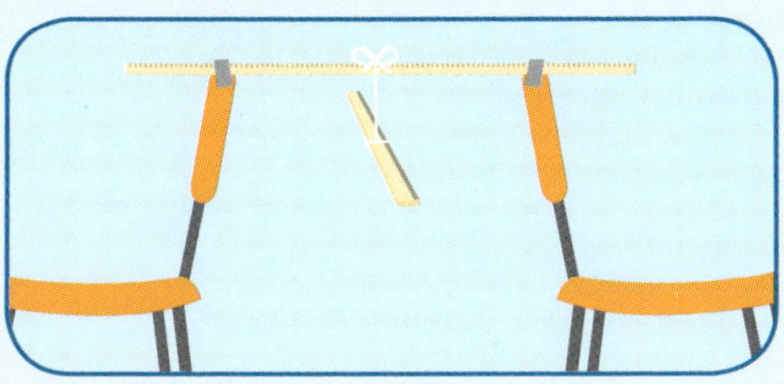

4 Use the pump to blow up the balloons. Make sure they are the same size.

5 Put a 3 cm piece of tape on the side of each balloon.

6 Tape the balloons to the ends of the second metre stick. Make sure the metre stick is balanced.

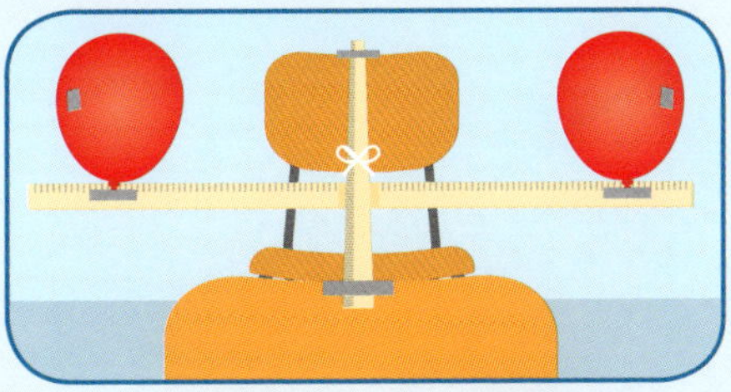

7 Push the pin through the piece of tape on one balloon. Pull the pin out.

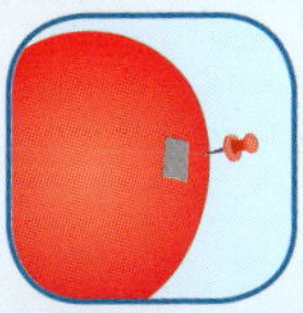

ANALYZE & REFLECT

1. What happened after you stuck the pin in the balloon?
2. Did you think that would happen? Why?

CHAPTER 2

FORCES OF FLIGHT

You can push on something.
You can pull on something.
A push or a pull is called a force.

There are four forces that work together to make airplanes fly.

Force LIFT

Lift is a force that pushes things up in the air. Lift can be very strong. When it is stronger than the weight of an object, lift pushes the object up in the air.

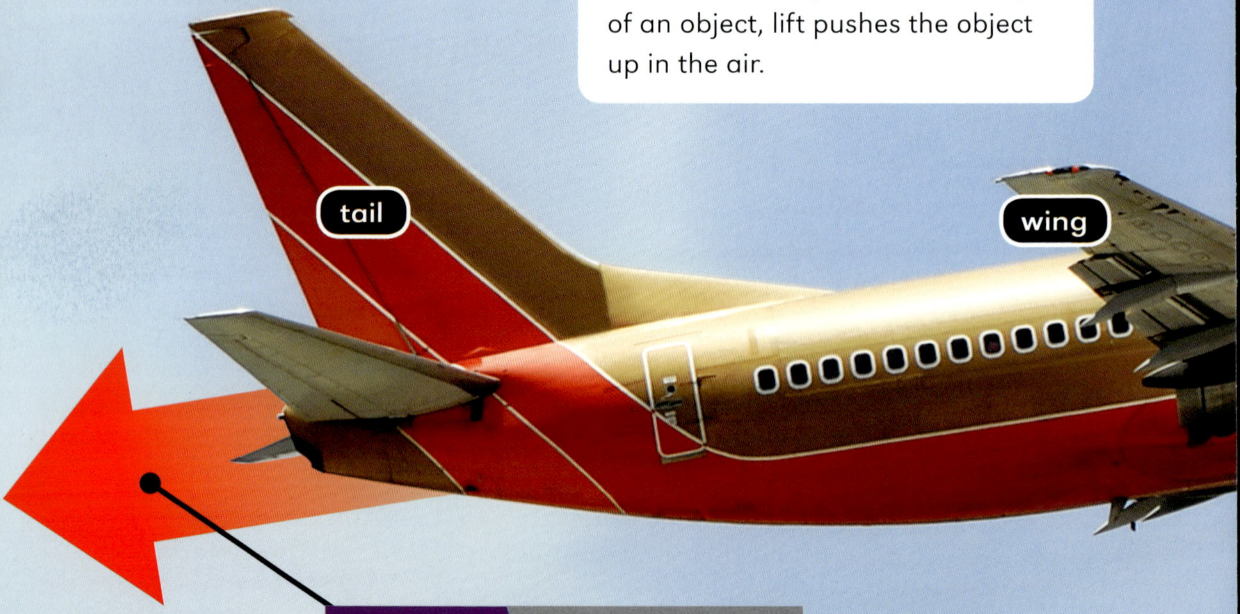

Force DRAG

Drag is a force that slows down something that is in the air. You feel drag when the wind pushes against you.

FYI

Everything that flies uses the four forces of flight. This includes birds and flying animals.

BIG IDEA There are four forces of flight. They are lift, drag, thrust, and weight.

Force THRUST

Thrust is a force that moves things in the air. It pushes or pulls things through the air.

Force WEIGHT

Gravity is a force that pulls things toward Earth. Gravity gives things weight. Your body's weight keeps you on the ground. Gravity pulls you down.

?

1. Which force slows something down?
2. Which force pulls something down?
3. Which forces keep airplanes in the air?

Weight and Lift

BIG IDEA Weight and lift are opposite forces.

Weight and lift are very different. They are opposites.
When a bird or an airplane is flying, weight and lift are equal.
When weight and lift are equal, we say they are balanced.

Weight pulls down.
Lift pushes up.

A bird uses its wings for lift.

Airplanes use their wings for lift.
Air moving over and under the wings produces lift.
The wings help airplanes rise and stay in the air.

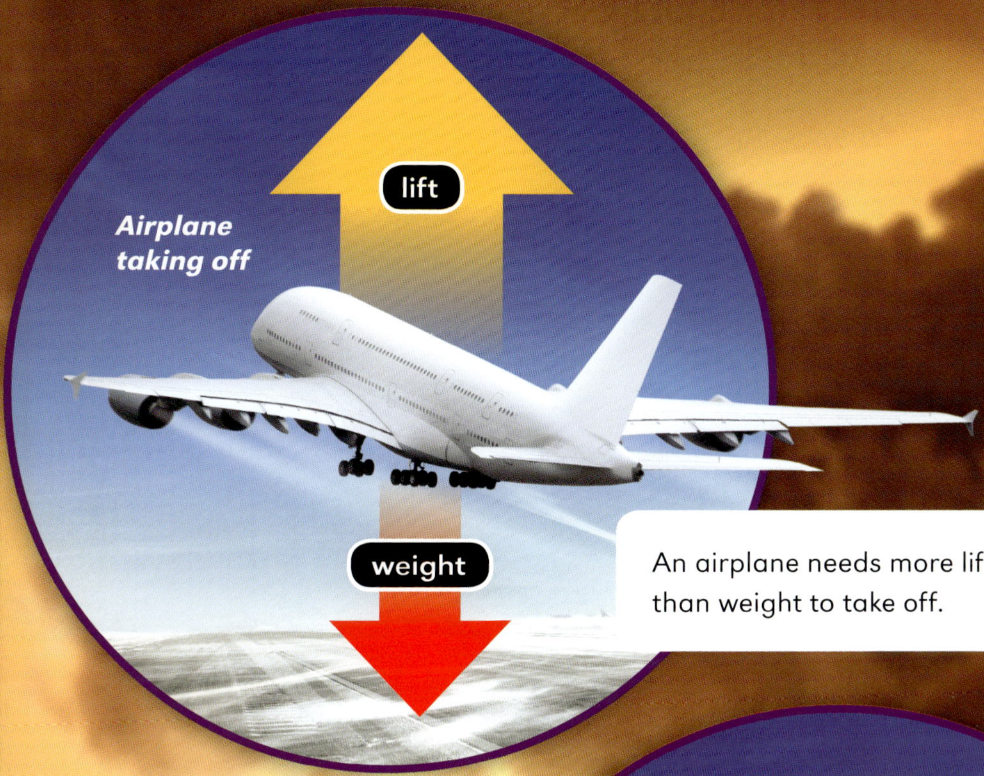

An airplane needs more lift than weight to take off.

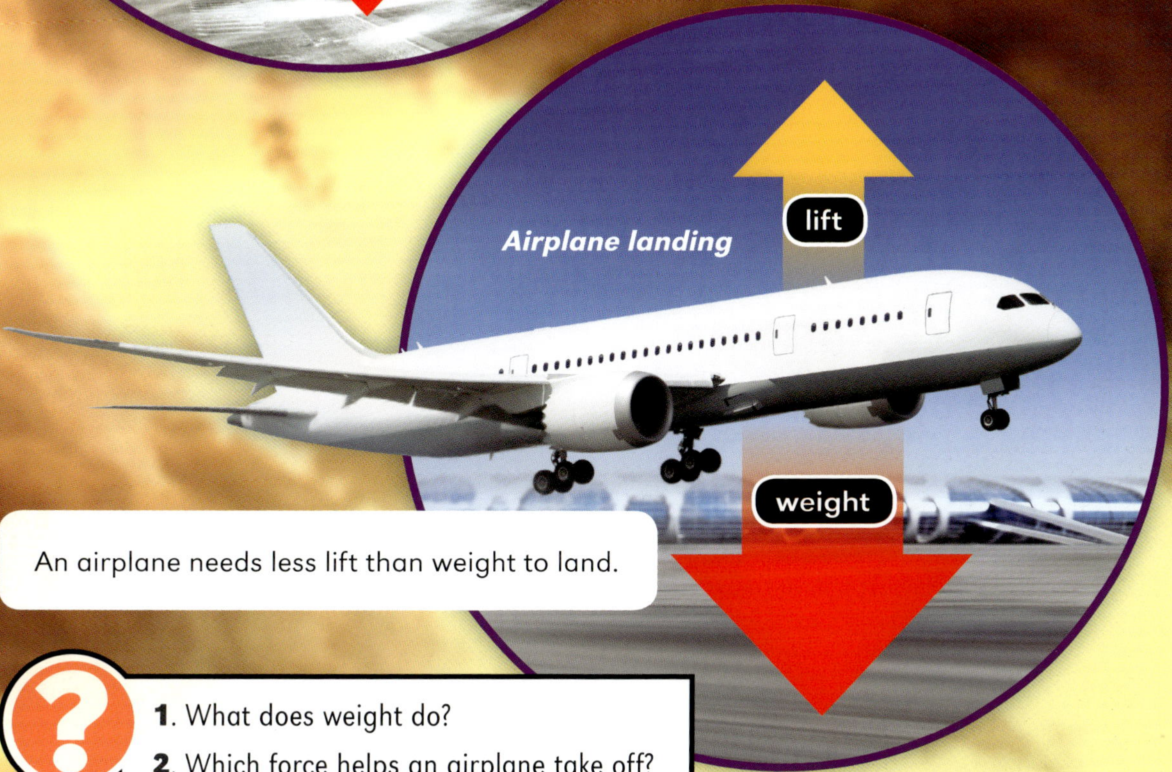

An airplane needs less lift than weight to land.

1. What does weight do?
2. Which force helps an airplane take off?

Drag and Thrust

BIG IDEA Drag and thrust are opposite forces.

Drag and thrust are very different. They are opposites. For a bird or an airplane to move forward, thrust must be greater than drag.

Drag slows down something that is moving. Thrust pushes or pulls something forward.

Some airplanes use propellers for thrust. Propellers pull the airplanes forward.

FYI

Pilots pull up the wheels when they are flying some airplanes. The wheels cause too much drag. The pilots put the wheels back down to land.

Jet engines pull in air at the front. Then they push air out the back. This gives the jet thrust. The jet moves forward.

An airplane needs more thrust than drag to take off.

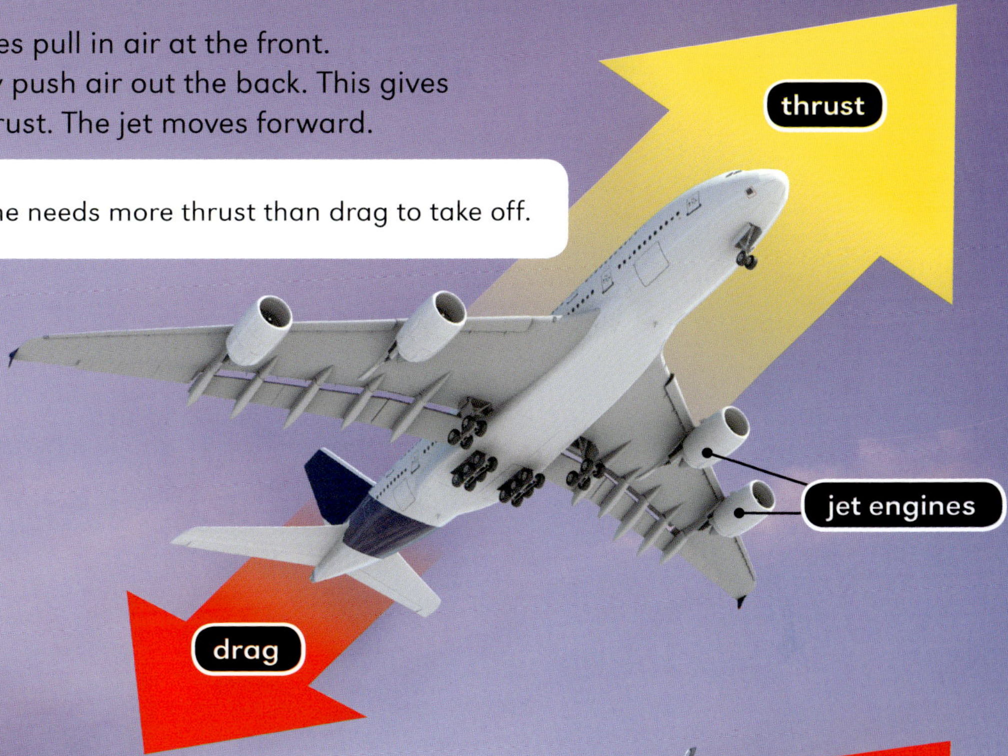

An airplane needs less thrust to land. Airplanes need drag to slow down after they land.

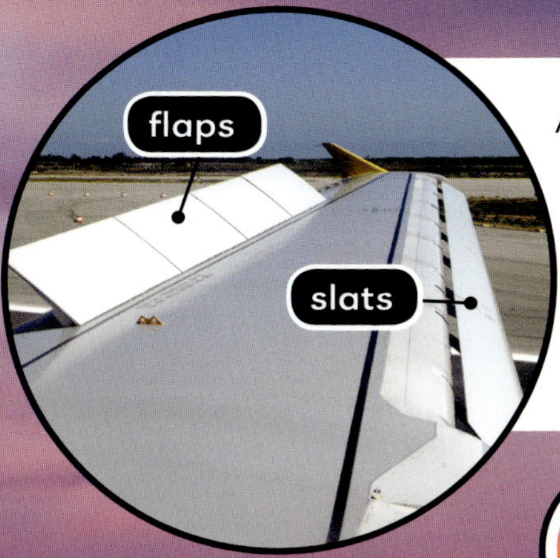

Airplane wings have slats and flaps. The pilot uses them to change how air moves around the wings to take off and land. When the front of the slats and the back of the flaps are down, there is more lift. There is also more drag.

1. What does drag do?

2. How does thrust help airplanes fly?

ACTIVITY 3

TEST GLIDERS

Make different gliders. Predict which one will work best.

YOU WILL NEED

blank paper

construction paper

aluminum foil

1 Predict which material will make the best glider. Record your prediction.

2 Choose one kind of paper. Fold down a 1 cm piece of the paper. Keep folding until you get to the middle of the paper.

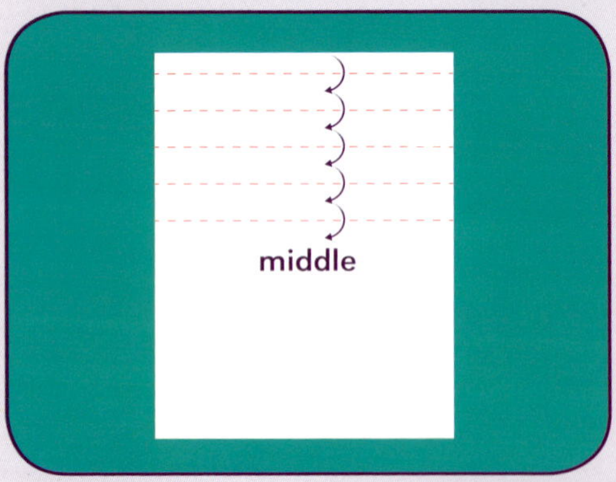

3 Fold the piece of paper the other way. Make the fold in the middle.

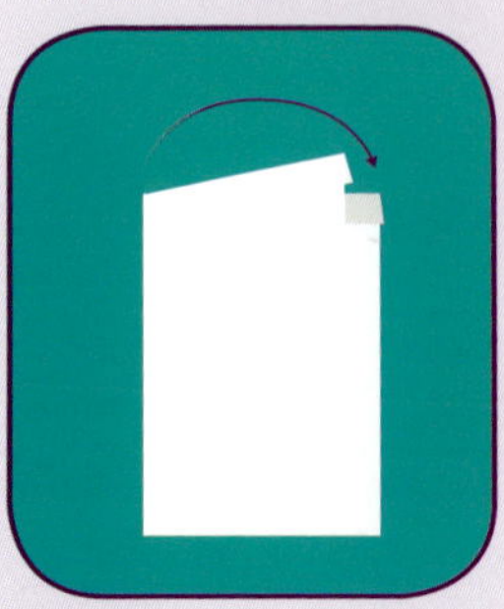

4 Fold the top layer of the paper back. Make sure the fold line is about 2 cm from the middle. Do the same to the other side.

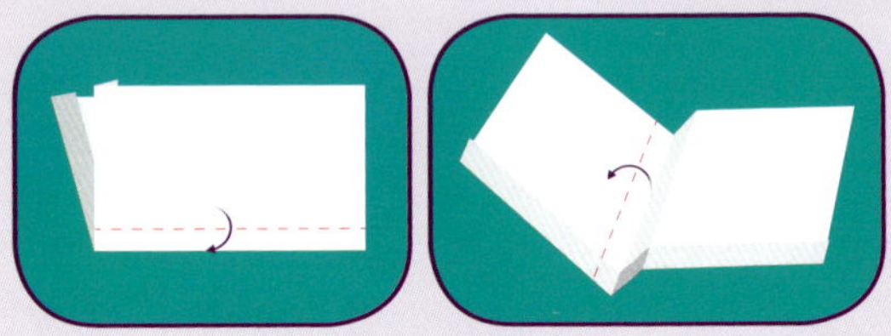

5 Hold your glider in the middle. The wings should stick out. Gently push your glider into the air. Record your observations.

6 Repeat steps 2–5 using the other materials.

BE SAFE

Do not fly your glider toward other people. It could harm their eyes.

ANALYZE & REFLECT

1. Which glider worked best? Was your prediction correct? Why did you make that prediction?
2. Why do you think your best glider worked best?

ACTIVITY 4

RESEARCH AND COMPARE

Make two different parachutes. Find out which one works better.

YOU WILL NEED

plastic bag

paper

string

small object

scissors

1 Make a parachute out of the plastic bag. Cut out a large hexagon.

2 Cut a small hole in each corner of the hexagon.

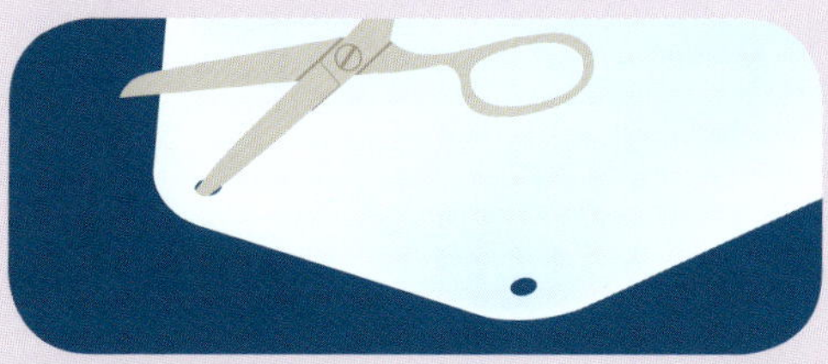

3 Cut six pieces of string. Each piece of string should be 40 cm long.

4 Tie each piece of string to a different hole in the hexagon.

5 Tie the other ends of the pieces of string to your small object.

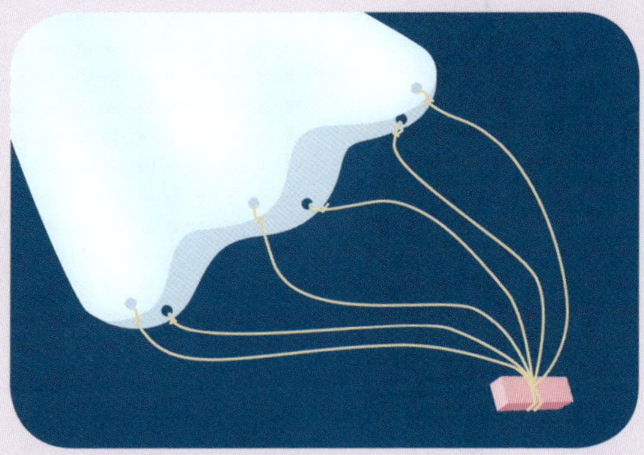

6 Test your parachute. Record your observations.

7 How could you make your parachute better? Could you use a different material? Could you change the size of the parachute? Make a plan. Write down your plan.

8 Build a new parachute using your plan. Repeat steps 6 and 7.

ANALYZE & REFLECT

1. Which parachute worked better? Why?
2. What else could you do to make your parachute work better?

CHAPTER 3

PEOPLE AND FL

What flying toys have you had fun flying?
Have you travelled in an airplane?
Where did you go?

We use flight to have fun.

We use flight to save lives.

IGHT

BIG IDEA Machines that fly have many different purposes.

We use flight to travel.

We use flight to explore space.

We use flight to fight forest fires.

1. For what other purposes do we use flight?
2. Which purpose for flight is the most important? Why?

Flight Has Changed Travel

BIG IDEA Flight has changed how people do things.

Our flying machines have changed over the years.

1909

The Silver Dart made the first flight in Canada. It flew around Baddeck Bay, Nova Scotia.

1913

H. W. Blakely flew an airplane with lights. It was the first airplane to fly at night in Canada.

WWI (1914–1918)

Canadian pilots flew airplanes like the Sopwith Camel in World War I.

FYI

Alexander Graham Bell studied flight. He worked with engineers to invent the Silver Dart.

1947

The Canadair North Star was the first passenger airplane built in Canada. It took people from Montreal, Quebec, to London, England.

Canadair North Star

1959

The Golden Hawks flying team trained in Chatham, New Brunswick. They flew at many air shows across Canada to entertain people.

Spitfire II

WWII (1939–1945)

Spitfire IIs were used in World War II.

Some Canadian women were pilots during WWII. They flew airplanes that carried mail and supplies.

Marion Orr was a Canadian WWII pilot.

TODAY

Many airplanes fly across Canada and to other countries around the world.

1. List some purposes for flight.
2. Which airplane was the most important? Why?

Flight and Our World

BIG IDEA Flight can be helpful and harmful.

Airplanes fly around the world every day. Flying helps people get to places fast. Flying helps people work around the world. But airplanes can be harmful in some ways.

Helpful

People can use airplanes to travel quickly to different countries.

Airplanes can get food and supplies quickly to people who need them.

The Canadian Red Cross flies supplies to people who need them.

Airplanes and helicopters can quickly transport people to hospitals.

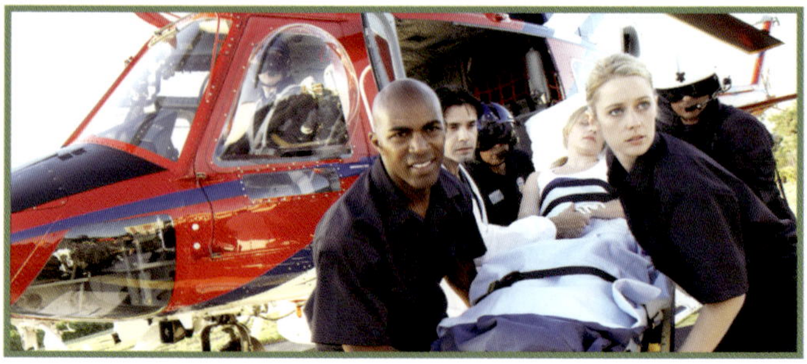

Harmful

Burning airplane fuel causes air pollution.

People who are sick may travel to another country by airplane. People in the country they visit may get sick.

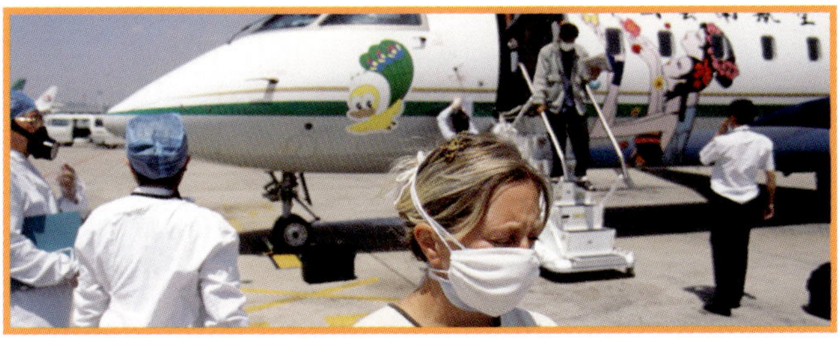

Airplanes make a lot of noise. The noise can bother people who live near airports.

Here are some ways to reduce the number of airplanes flying.

People can take a train to travel to some places.

People can eat food that is grown in the area where they live.

People can use video calls to have meetings.

1. How can flight be helpful? How can it be harmful?
2. In what other ways can people reduce the number of airplanes flying?
3. Reducing the number of airplanes would cut down on pollution. What might be some problems with reducing the number of airplanes?

ACTIVITY 5

RECORD HOW YOU USE FLIGHT

Draw a picture to show a time when you used flight.

1 Think of a time when you used flight.
Did you fly a glider or a parachute? Did you fly a kite?
Did you let go of a floating balloon?

2 Draw a picture of what you did.

3 Write a few sentences about your picture.

ANALYZE & REFLECT

1. Add labels to your picture for lift, drag, thrust, and weight.
2. What other ways would you like to use flight?

ACTIVITY 6

FIND OUT ABOUT JOBS IN FLIGHT

Some people need to know about flight to do their jobs. What jobs are these people doing?

1

2

3

4

1 Look at each photo.

2 What job does each photo show?

3 Write a sentence about each job. What might each person need to know about flight?

ANALYZE & REFLECT

1. Which job would you like to do?

2. Write about why you would like to do that job.

THINK LIKE AN ENGINEER
TO DESIGN PAPER AIRPLANES

Make two different paper airplanes. Use what you know about the forces of flight to make your airplanes do tricks.

YOU COULD USE

- regular white paper
- large white paper
- tape
- index card
- construction paper
- hula hoop

1 Make two different paper airplanes.

2 Try to make them do the tricks below. Try each trick three times.

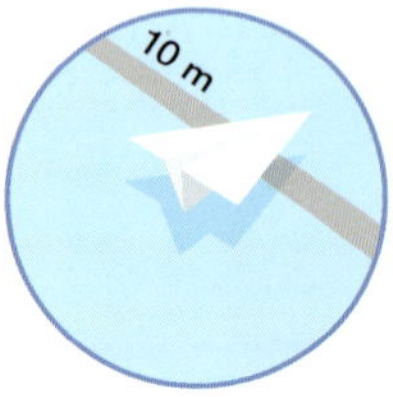

Fly 10 m before touching the ground.

Fly through a hula hoop.

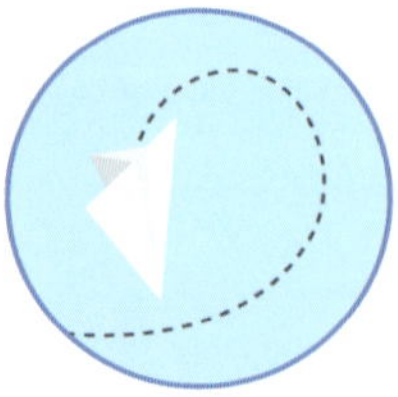

Make a loop in the air.

Stay in the air for three seconds.

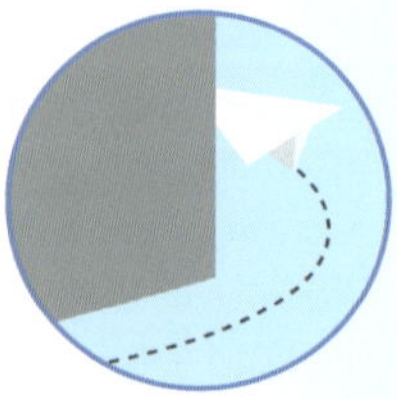

Turn around a corner.

3 How did you use what you know about flight to design your paper airplanes?
Why did you choose the paper you used?
How did your airplanes get thrust?
How did your airplanes get lift?
Did you use drag? How?
Which airplane worked better? Why?

BE SAFE

Do not fly your paper airplane at other people. It could harm their eyes.

COMMUNICATE

1 Draw a picture of your best paper airplane design. Show it doing one of the tricks. Label your picture to show how the design helped your airplane do the trick.

2 Compare your picture of your paper airplane design with a classmate's picture. Talk about how you could make an even better paper airplane. Try making it and flying it.

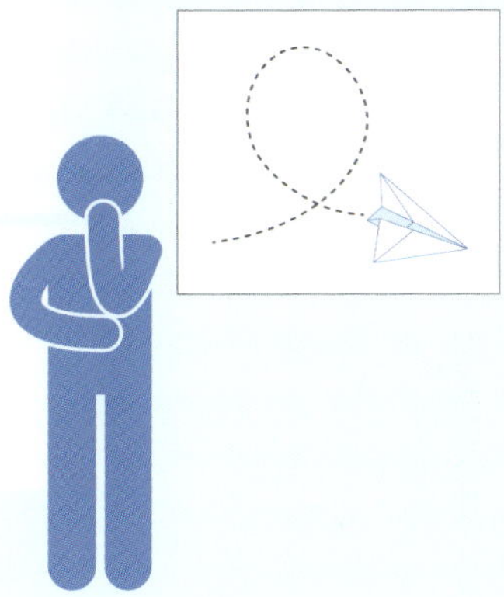

VOCABULARY

1 Write out the four forces of flight. Draw a picture to explain each force. Explain your pictures to a classmate. Answer his or her questions about your pictures.

2 Make a list of the helpful things about flight. Make another list of the harmful things about flight. Are the helpful things about flight more important than the harmful things about flight? Write a sentence to explain your thoughts.

Helpful	Harmful
fast	pollution

REVIEW

Talk about these questions with a classmate.

1. What is the difference between air close to Earth and air high above Earth?
2. How can you make air molecules spread out to make the air less dense?
3. How does a hot-air balloon rise?
4. What are the four forces of flight?
5. Which forces of flight are opposites?
6. Which forces does an airplane use to land?
7. When have you used flight?
8. What are some helpful things about flight?
9. What are some harmful things about flight?
10. What is the biggest change in people's use of flight over the years?

Glossary

design
(dih-zyne)
make a plan for building something

equal
(ee-kwuhl)
the same in size or amount

hexagon
(hek-suh-gon)
a shape with six sides

opposite
(op-uh-sit)
completely different

pollution
(puh-loo-shuhn)
something that makes the land, air, or water harmful to people and other living things

predict
(prih-dikt)
use your knowledge to decide what will likely happen

record
(rih-kord)
write something down

reduce
(rih-doos)
use less of a material

vent
(vent)
an opening that lets air, gas, or liquid go out of a container or room

Index